BY ANNA V. EPELBAUM

MATHEMATICS

VOLUME I

FROM ZERO LEVEL TO SUCCESSFUL SCORES ON ANY STANDARDIZED TEST

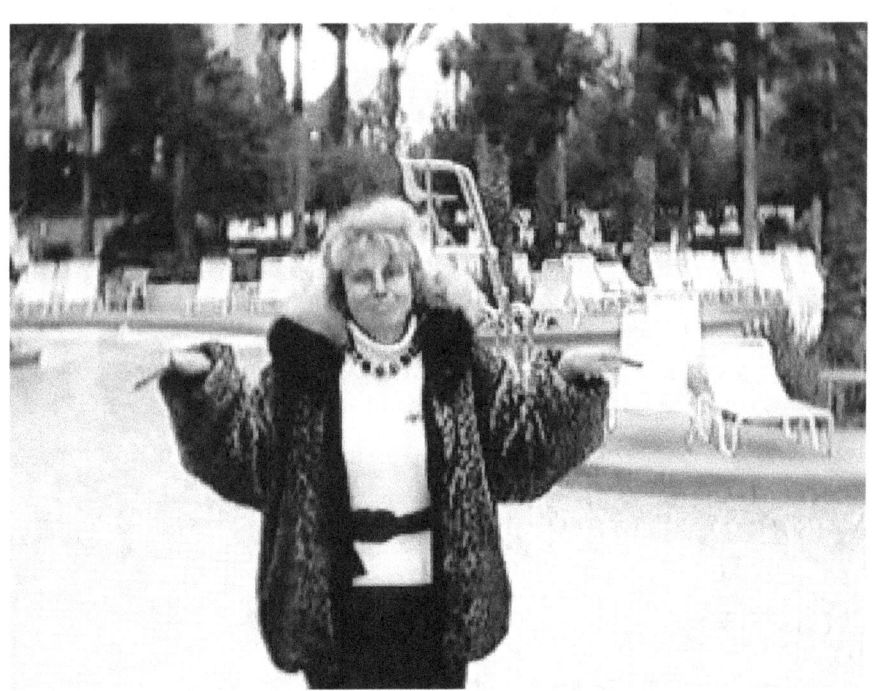

INTRODUCTION

This book doesn't pretend to change curricula. The main goal of this book to fill in the gaps between what is taught in high school, and what is required by educational standards for high school graduates in the area of mathematics.

This book should be very useful for both high school and junior college students. It should be very useful for adults who want to get their GED. It can be also very useful for high school mathematics teachers who want to refresh their teaching skills, and, maybe, even for professors of mathematics, who, for whatever reason, don't have a solid background in the foundation mathematics, and, therefore, have difficulties in their creative scientific activities.

The book consists of two parts:

Volume I covers everything from zero level of mathematical knowledge to a sufficient level of knowledge to successfully pass SAT and ACT tests. This book includes six separate mini-courses: 1. Word Problems, 2. Arithmetic, 3. Algebra, 4. Geometry and Trigonometry, 5. Functions and Graphs, 6. Sets, Statistics, and Probability.

Specific emphasis is made in the book on correct usage of calculators (both a simple calculator, and a scientific, graphing calculator), and all theoretical knowledge that students need to possess in order to use them. Course Word Problems introduces the language of tests, other courses provide knowledge.

Volume II covers material from successful scores in basic ACT and SAT tests up to the entrance requirements of the most sophisticated colleges and universities. This volume includes six courses - the advanced continuation of the courses of Volume I, and an Appendix, which presents some sophisticated, and very educational problems (with solutions) to illustrate goals set by Volume II's six courses.

Both books have numerous examples, many of which are taken from SAT, ACT, SAT I, SAT II, SAT III tests of previous years to illustrate all materials covered by these books in their order of presentation.

Consequently, these books provide all of the theoretical explanation, and often their precise proofs, that students need in order to understand, and utilize all of the areas of mathematics knowledge and mastery that are required by official curricula.

The author of this book received her mathematical training and initial teaching experience in the special mathematical high school, organized, and supervised by the Mathematical Faculty of the Moscow State University, then was graduated from this Mathematical Department of the Moscow State University, teaching simultaneously in the high school of her own origin and other similar facilities, while receiving her graduate degrees from the Moscow State University. Then she taught in this school of her initial origin full time, while teaching part time on graduate level before she received her own Ph. D in Applied Mathematics. She intensively used in this book this part of her training and teaching experience, as well as, her further teaching experience in Austria, Italy, and in the USA on college and secondary school levels.

So, let us begin with the initial test. This way each reader can check himself/herself.

The Introductory Test

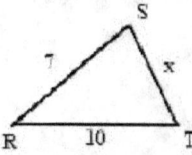

Incorrect answer leads to GEOMETRY & TRIGONOMETRY

A) $3 <= p <= 17$
B) $3 <= p <= 20$
C) $17 <= p <= 20$
D) $17 <= p <= 34$
E) $20 <= p <= 34$

Correct answer is E.

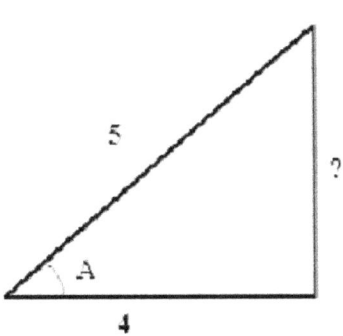

2.

Given triangle is right. The length of one leg is 4, the hypotenuse is 5. What is the value of sin(A), cos(A) & ctg(A) subsequently?

A) 4/5; 3/5; 3/4
B) 3/5; 4/5; 4/3
C) 3/5; 4/5; 3/4
D) 4/5; 3/5; 4/3
Correct answer is B. Incorrect answer leads to TRIGONOMETRY.

3. The graph of f(x) is shown below.

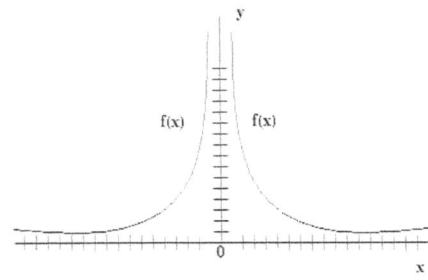

Which of the following could be a domain of f ?

A) {x: x<> 0}
B) {x: x> 0 }
C) { x: x> 1 }
D) { x: x>=1 }

Correct answer is A. Incorrect answer leads to FUNCTIONS & GRAPHS.

4. If it is true that every precious stone is harder than glass, which of the following statements is correct?

    A) Glass can be a precious stone.
    B) Every stone harder than glass is a precious stone.
    C) Every stone softer than glass is not a precious stone.
    D) Some stones softer than glass are precious stones.

Correct answer is C. Incorrect answer leads to WORD PROBLEMS.

5. Cynthia, Peter, Kevin, and Nancy are tailors. Each of them made following number of skirts within previous month:

    Cynthia -36
    Peter -   45
    Nancy - 14
    Kevin - 13

What is the average number for this month?

    A) 39
    B) 42
    C) 27
    D) 25

Correct answer is C. A failure leads to ARITHMETIC.

6. What is the negative solution of an equation $x^2 - 4x + 4 = 0$?

    A) 1
    B) 2
    C) -2
    D) -1
    E) None of the above

Correct answer is E. None of the above. A failure leads to Algebra.

7. What is a value of $(3/5 - 1/4)$? Is it a decimal number?
    A) 0.35; Yes.
    B) 7/20; No
    C) 7/20; Yes
    D) Both A&C

Correct answer is D. Both A & C. A failure leads to ARITHMETIC.

8. Set A contains only the factors of 21 that are greater than 1, and set B contains only the factors of 48 that are greater than 1. If set C is the union of sets A and B, what is the mode of set C?

    A) 2
    B) 3
    C) 8
    D) 12
E. Set C has no mode.

Correct answer is B. Incorrect result leads to SETS, STATISTICS & PROBABILITY.

9. If $a + b = 7$ and $a^2 + b^2 = 37$, then what is the value of ab?

    A) 6
    B) 12
    C) 15
    D) 22

Correct answer is A. A failure leads to the course ALGEBRA.

10. If someone needs to cover the same distance , moving with constant speed, the time of his journey and his speed are in indirect variation. If walking with a speed
6 km/hour, someone needs 5 hours for the whole journey. What will be the speed of his car, if he covers this distance by car within one hour?
How long is this distance?

    A) 30 km/hour; 30 km.
    B) 1.2 km/hour; 1.2 km.
    C) 30 km/hour; 6 km.
    D) 20 km/hour; 25 km.

Correct answer is A. Incorrect answer leads to ALGEBRA, SETS , STATISTICS....
& FUNCTIONS AND GRAPHS.

11. Roberto travels from his home to the beach driving at 30 mph. He returns along the same route at 50 mph. If the distance from Roberto's house to the beach is ten miles, then what is Roberto's average speed for the round trips miles per hour.

    A) 32.5
    B) 37.5
    C) 40.0
    D) 42.5
    E) 45.5

    Correct answer is B.

Link to ALGEBRA, SETS & STATISTICS & PROBABILITY.
    Now after you check yourself out you can start to read and to perform training of our courses in the order they are presented by this book, or in the order, which is determined by your test's results.
    So, go ahead, folks!!

Content of the first volume

WORD PROBLEMS

Introduction.

Mathematics is a language of science. In order to solve any of real world problems, someone needs at the first place to describe this problem correctly, and then translate this description from common language into language of science, assuming that he/she knows all technical tools (formulas and mathematical methods) to solve these problems.

All other courses of these branch are devoted to the development of the mathematical technique for solutions.

This course is devoted to the problems' set up - the translation of problems from English into the language of math.

We also shall refresh in this course some basic knowledge of Physics, Geometry, Numbers Theory, Set's Theory, and money's calculations, which are assumed as familiar by standard ACT, SAT I & SAT II tests.
This course also provides a wide range of examples, and three real time scale tests, which include all types of possible word problems utilized in SAT & ACT tests within last four years.

The Content of the Course

ARITHMETIC

Arithmetic Introduction

Maybe, you think that there is no problem to calculate anything you want to calculate because you can always use a calculator.

It is not true. You need basic skills to use any device.

You, certainly need basic arithmetic skills to be ready to use a calculator correctly.

Let us take a very simple example:

$$3 + 3 * 5 + 14 / 2 = ?$$

You do not need even to know anything about fractions to calculate this example. However, if you do not know what the order of arithmetic operations means, you will get a wrong result either with or without a calculator. In this case, a wrong result could be 37, for example, if you do not know the order of arithmetic operators. The current result is 25.

Therefore, in this course we will cover all areas of arithmetic required by ACT, SAT I & SAT II tests. After the completion of this course, you will be able to calculate any arithmetic problem no matter with or without a calculator. You also shall be able to use a calculator successfully for solution of much more complicated problems, which anyone usually cannot perform sufficiently without a calculator, computer, tables of logarithm, etc.

Content of Course

ALGEBRA

Introduction.

Algebra is the most required part of the high school math.

As we are doing it with all other courses of these mathematical series, this first course covers only topics, which are required for SAT and ACT. If someone wants to be successful with SAT II, and college entrance tests, it is necessary, sure, to take

ALGEBRA I in addition to this course. This course is included in Part II of our book. However, we are trying in this current course to show how to solve pretty difficult problem, which theoretical part covered by the content of it. Most likely, this kind of problems can appear in the advanced tests like SAT II, etc.

In the ALGEBRA I course we cover topics that are not required by SAT and ACT. These topics are required by SAT II. We solve subsequently problems based on these topics, and teach the most advanced technique of problems' solution.

Algebra is a very old science and its gems have lost their charms for us through everyday usage. We have tried by this course to refresh them for our students.

It is necessary to do because algebra is used in everyday's life more than any other part of math. Okay. Let us start.

Content of Course

GEOMETRY &TRIGONOMETRY

Introduction.

Geometry is second after algebra, the most important part of the high school mathematics. There are different geometry's known to mathematicians. We are studying here the geometry created by Euclid. This geometry appeared earlier than others and is, therefore, more developed than others.

Traditionally geometry is a part of math, which teaches students to think sequentially and logically, to set up and prove theorems on the basis of initial postulates (axioms), then to set up and prove a new set of theorems on the basis of first step theorems, etc.

Students are not required by SAT`s, SAT II, and even college entrance`s tests to be able to prove theorems. Therefore, we show them in this course as examples. We are not proving here everything, but students must understand that, as we already mention in the course Word Problems, the ability to set up and especially to prove theorems correctly is very close to the ability to set up and to solve different word problems. Therefore, students, who want to be successful with word problems, should pay explicit attention to everything, which is connected with the formal aspects of theorems, and their proofs.

As we mentioned above, we covered in this course requirements of ACT, SAT, and SAT 1. The extension of this course, which covers SAT II (all levels) and possible requirements of entrance tests' in the most advanced colleges is offered by the course Geometry and Trigonometry I.

Content of Course

FUNCTIONS & GRAPHS

Introduction.

     This course is created to make students familiar with method of coordinates, the definitions of functions, and main features of the number of specific functions, which are considered in high school mathematics and required by SAT, ACT, and SAT I tests.

     You can tell us that a graphing calculator can do all this work for you. You are wrong. You can't use a graphing calculator successfully without basic knowledge of functions the same way as you can't use successfully a simple calculator without basic arithmetic and algebraic knowledge. We will show you in this course what you need to ask from a graphing calculator, and we teach you here how to solve problems, if you don't have a graphing calculator all of a sudden.

     As usually, we offer the continuation of this course **Functions and Graphs I.** This additional course covers the biggest part of pre-calculus and also make you able to operate in four dimensional space as it is required by the modern physics. This additional course introduces some other coordinate systems, which you are expected to use in college **Calculus** courses.

Content of Course

SETS, STATISTICS &

PROBABILITY

"The true logic of this world is in the calculus of probabilities."

-James Clerk Maxwell

Introduction

This course seems to be not as important for SAT, SAT I, and ACT as Algebra or Geometry. As a matter of fact, students don't study on the regular basis in high school statistics and probability. You, sure, shall need it in everyday life and especially in science and technology not less than other branches of math.

We want to emphasize here that your success in **The Science Reasoning test** tremendously dependent on your fluency in the matherial of this course. Even if this course is practically the shortest of our basic courses because, as we mentioned above, this subject is not explicitly taught in high school, the course **Sets, Statistics, and Probability I** is designed to provide you all necessary knowledge to operate, for example, with our six advanced courses of Physics, which should prepare you for requirements of most advanced institutions in this area, or with any other advanced subjects' courses by your own choice.

Therefore, let us start.

Sets, Statistics, and Probability
Index

That is all for now, folks!!

The introduction of the second part of this course looks like following:

We introduce in this course. normal Gauss distribution, and Poisson distribution. We introduce here also Marcow chains and the law of "large numbers". We talk a bit about stochastic process, and how you can plan an experiment.

We introduce the Heisenberg uncertainty principle and its math basis. Detailed explanations and many examples, which are provided here, as in all our other courses to illustrate all steps of explanation, shall make for you a good acquaintance and even a friendship with the dark queen of mathematics - Probability.

TUTORIALS ARE AVAILACLE FOR ADDITIONAL
CHARGE

CONTACT OVER (217-359-3619) OR

OVER www.moscowtochicago.com

BOTH VOLUMES IN COLOR COULD BE ALSO
PURCHASED ON www.lulu.com & www.moscowtochicago.com

www.ingramcontent.com/pod-product-compliance
Lightning Source LLC
Chambersburg PA
CBHW081248170526
45165CB00009B/3247

9 781438 254487